ISLANDS LOVELIER THAN A VISION

D1364576

Cyril Dabydeen

Peepal Tree Press

First published 1986
Peepal Tree Press
53, Grove Farm Crescent
Leeds LS16 6BZ
Yorkshire
England

ISBN 0 948833 02 5

INTRODUCTION

In Canada and the Caribbean, Cyril Dabydeen, as an established poet and writer of fiction, needs no introduction. However, since little of his work has reached Britain, a brief note is in order.

Dabydeen grew up in the rural Corentyne district of Guyana, but attended school at Queen's Royal College in the capital, Georgetown. He taught in Guyana between 1961-1970. Even in his early adolescence, however, his real ambition was to be a writer; during his youth he read widely in the works of such Caribbean writers as Mittelholzer, Wilson Harris, Lamming, Naipaul and Roger Mais. His first published poems began to appear during the 1960s in Guyanese journals such as *New World Fortnightly* and *Kaie;* he received several of Guyana's most prestigious poetry prizes for this work. His poems from this period were collected in *Poems in Recession* which was published by Sheik Sadeek in 1972.

Poems in Recession speaks of a commitment to socialism, nation-building, and an intense effort to understand the inter-ethnic racism and growing tendency towards authoritarianism which gnawed at the possibilities of a new freedom in Guyana. But there is also an intoxification with language and image which indicates that Dabydeen's impulses were towards intenser forms of poetic self-expression. He records that as one who was not of the middle class, he knew that this kind of self-fulfilment as a writer could not be found in Guyana. Indeed, as the adolescent reader of Naipaul and Lamming, he had already been seized by the idea of the 'writer's self-exile' and that 'if one wanted to write, one had to go abroad.' One suspects that lurking behind all Dabydeen's work is the feeling that were it not for the gifts which made him a writer, he would have been condemned to the idleness and ignorance of the rural youths of his village. He writes of a character trying to escape from village futility through a show of Hindu punditry in his first, satirical novel, *The Wizard Swami,* completed in 1972, but not published until 1984 (Calcutta Writers' Workshop).

In 1970 he left for Canada, a place whose cool contrasts with the heat of his Corentyne village had been part of his boyish consciousness. His first years in Northern Ontario were spent in the archetypal mythological Canadian activites of tree-planting and living in bush camps with 'Native Indians, trappers, miners, alcoholics and hoboes.' Later he took a first degree in English and Masters in English and Public Administration.

Through the example of the novelist Austin Clarke, he began to see the difficult possibilities of being a West Indian writer in Canada, of attempting to become embedded in Canada (he is now a Canadian citizen) whilst recognising that his sensibility had been formed in the Caribbean. He has been intensely aware of the dangers of being a writer confined to the ghetto of marginality and racism in Canadian society and his work deals both with the themes of 'immigration and discrimination' and of the expanding conciousness'. To some extent his fiction, so far, has dealt with the social realities of the former; *Still Close To The Islands* (1982) is a collection of harsh and spare stories of Guyanese rural poverty and the alienation of the immigrant in Canada. His collections of poetry, *Distances* (1972, Fiddlehead Poetry Books), *Goatsong* (1977, Mosaic Press), *This Planet Earth* (1979, Borealis Press), *Heart's Frame* (1979, Vesta Publications) and *Elephants Make Good Stepladders* (1982, Third Eye Publications) combine both his acute sense of social reality and his desire to explore the 'bottomless pool of origins', looking past the urban immigrant experience of Canada, the rural settler experience of the Indo-Guyanese, and the ancestral images of India for the 'elemental man'.

His work in Canada has found widespread recognition and praise. His poems and short stories have appeared in countless journals and numerous anthologies. Through awards and grants given in recognition of his work he has been able to travel widely, to Europe, Cuba and South America. In 1985 he was appointed Poet Laureate of Ottawa.

Other Books by Cyril Dabydeen :

(POETRY)

Poems in Recession *(Sadeek Press: Georgetown, Guyana, 1972)*
Distances *(Fiddlehead Poetry Books: University of New Brunswick, 1977)*
Goatsong *(Mosaic Press: Oakville, Ontario, 1977)*
Heart's Frame *(Vesta Publications: Cornwall, Ontario, 1979)*
This Planet Earth *(Borealis Press: Ottawa, 1979)*
Elephants Make Good Stepladders *(Third Eye Publications: London, Ontario, 1982)*

(FICTION)

Still Close to the Island *(Commoners Press: Ottawa, 1980)*

CONTENTS

I

II

III

IV

Let me reach the bright day, the high chair, the plain desk, where my hand at last controls the words, where anxiety no longer undermines me. If I don't reach these I'm thrown to the wolves, I'm a restless animal wandering from place to place, from experience to experience.

Stephen Spender, *Notebooks.*

I
... the meandering self

LEGENDS

I

I begin my book of legends
to be other than I am.
I walk across the high bridge,
barefooted in the blistering sun.
I swelter, seeking shelter
from overhanging trees.

Dismay follows with a young
bull bellowing; my father's lasso
converges. He looks back
as I imagine an outside life—
fishing in Ontario, skiing down
Vancouver mountains
from glossy magazines.

I am still on the winding path,
looking for retreat once in awhile.
I continue to be livid,
I take further note of the sun.

II

Later in Canada, amidst deciduous
trees, I test myself: I am in a
muskeg, hounded by blackflies
and mosquitoes. I plant tree after tree.
I brace against the cold in northern
Ontario—freezing one more time.

III

In Kingston I am a founding father
living up to treaties; I bolster
with the old fort: I nurture defence
with brittle skin and flesh;
I grimace as guns keep
firing in my head.

IV

In Ottawa I am Governor General
and Prime Minister, too,
Parliament Hill my domain. I look
around: cannons firing from the past,
relived in my dreams. A burning next.
I continue to listen to entreaties.
War Measures Act. My mind festering
solitudes.

V

Finally, my mother, to remind me
of myself, sends a postcard from
Tobago—she on her first holiday
after fifty years or more.
I continue to make humming noises
in my sleep

CHANGING

I gather the heat
in all my cells
I forge with every ounce of flesh

I splay out on the ground
scattering organs, blood
everywhere

I gather them up again
for a renewed self
I plaster everything with wax

Suddenly I begin to fly—
I am Icarus
venturing out—

in, then down
as I am still aloft
singing in the tunnels

of my flesh, the corridors
of heart and lungs
in my hollow bones

I moult, bird-like
anew, as never before
heart pulsating—

my future's self
again aloft
in the frenzy of breathing

BACKYARD & TENEMENT

Where the night lures
    and the sun sets too quickly—
where the old woman with corrugated face
    gnarled in more places than one—
her face like the tenement
    she has lived in all these years

    her grandson daily conspiring
to throw a lasso
    round the moon, bringing it down
and stepping over it—
    where the voodooienne strides
by my side
    ready for the haunting

This zombie craze in my life
    by old St Patrick's Anglican—
where a malnourished niece falls victim
    to more than plantation lore
& a headmaster suggests urine-magic –
    the eternal cure

So the legendary Dutch-man in me reappears
    wishing to be buried once again
with a slave as assurance of the after-life
    —never really dying
    being more sepulchral than tombs
and rife with chains rattling

blood yet dripping from my skin
in the ball o' fire dark

DROWNING CATS

There is really nothing to it—
it happens in Belfast too, where they
also have their poor, the ghettoes:
it's like singing sad songs
with tattered clothes flapping in the wind

The cats meowing in the darkness, all
night long, awakening a young girl who will
rise early the next morning to prepare food
for her husband ready to go to the canefields—
another kind of whimpering, if you like

The cat's disdain, its eyes livid in the semi-dark
then emerald and neon; you wait and watch,
fearing the kittens that are soon to be born—
sometimes half a dozen or more. In a year, maybe,
scores will be staring at you in the streets,
as you walk by with fish in hand

The days go by, the nights also whimpering.
Grandmother would repeat:
"Now there's really nothing to it;
simply put them in a bag and tie the end.
They will not see, they will not remember—
how to get back here."

Funnily enough, so often they seem to return—
these same cats, like a haunting, familiar
as old memories

My girlfriend casually tells me that in Belfast
they also do the same—maybe with a difference:
they tie the bag with a stone
and drown them

THIS FATHER'S LIFE

This father's life I plunge into
surfacing with the dream of cattle
a hinterland's jaguar-call
a grunt as good as a bray

A coastland voice next
as I am memory of the deciphering madness
I walk around, pulverizing
with distress—

going back with a thousand images,
song of siren, expecting
something new to be born
a calf's head jutting out
a branding three months later

I am the squeal and the running hooves
I am the beast tearing out entrails
from the mouth-shape of a tree
I am the howl against the moon
in a father's sun-absence

where gall and bitter dew-drop
make for memory much too long

MY BROTHER IS A HERO

He rummages through the forest
with a passion
he tears whole trees down
with a savagery that is livid in nightmares

He builds chairs, tables, cabinets—
he's galvanized more than zinc
he's the turbulence of tropical sun & rain

he heaves and toils with frenzy
and the forest more than Macbeth's
moves at his command

new things are born from day to day
more trees with arms & legs
he spins the landscape around
he's a maker first of all

with sawdust blood & bones

STILL LIFE

Hear her,
With her lips sealed
From afar
You could tell she was swinging
A chicken by the neck
With blood squirting from her fingers,
Like rain

With thunder in her eyes,
She breathed out moonshine
She who could ferret out lightning
By baring her teeth
In the virulent sun

How she laughed—
    she was still young then,
Full of energy, like a young horse
    One afternoon, I remember
She brought home a lover
And wrapped her arms about him
    like wet banana leaves

I was under the house
    built on stilts, then
Playing Robin Hood & his Merrymen
    amidst tropical sun & rain
    I was also Errol Flynn
Making Captain Blood arches
    dazzling with a sword
In the guise of skull
    & crossbones

THE HUSBAND

After a week
In the town's brothel
He came home
Bringing Shamin, the town whore
With him

His fat wife (she was once beautiful
With fair skin)
Sat in the kitchen and grumbled
By herself

I, one of the villagers, gossiped
Like the rest
While he remained
In the bedroom upstairs
In the house built
On stilts

His wife knew there
Was nothing she could do
But wait until his passion
Was sated
            —with a bottle of rum

She muttered about leaving him
But she never really did—
        "It was bound to happen that way,"
I heard her once say
        to her children

Afterwards he played
        the mandolin beautifully—
His wife laughed
        all by herself

MY SUNDRY LIFE

My sundry life
I've given over
to wielding in a storm
with pellets of rain
        —and everywhere
the meandering self in green

I murmur regret
        in an alligator-creek
with star-shaped ripples
        I bend and circle—
a dogfish flotilla
        in my midst
scattering fragments of the sun

Glinting more of my life
        with thunder-belch
and forest-spell
        I listen with continuing awe
pressing an ear to the ground
        my heart beating further rain

Such is my beloved,
        my eyes plastered
with clay—
a memory song once again
        my sounds of soil & floating things
in the everlasting presence
        of dreams gone haywire
on this one-time
        homing ground

REFUGEE

I give you Canada,
sisters & brothers
I give you whole skyscrapers
the tumbling down of concrete next
come here do not leave
hold on to the busyness of airports
escalators will grip you like sweet
tropical perfumes when you are no longer
close to the sea
everything will fade after a while
old memories, old faces : mark my words
do not doubt me
enter the subway and hold on tightly—
here it is perfect restfulness
you will sleep soundly after the first night
no hum, no whir – the darkness is all
in Mississauga not far from Toronto
in an airport hotel Air Canada pays for

I will sign a bond for you, I will talk my guts out
tell lies to Immigration officials
so you will get locked up safely
in an apartment all winter
remember the beautiful sun?
ah, here too is paradise if you can bear it
do not forget to dream of a vacation
once every five years perhaps

will you go underground and tell lies?
falsify a social security card
because you want to work hard
make cabinets, chairs, beds
fill your hands with foam like so much fluff
and make-believe that you're still in the clouds?

your wife is pregnant, brother,
the disc of sun in her uterus
the yowling of cats and ululation of dogs
centuries behind

offsprings have ways of inhabiting a land
of putting sticks & stones together
of hurling them across an ocean
in a ship's galley in the indentured furrows of a land
where a sugar plantation is at ease—
sip tea with me and enjoy more of paradise

I love you all, even with the breathing hard
of an asthmatic old woman
by your side in dire distress
take Canada with you, deep in your veins

make the land intimately yours
one day you will tell your sons & daughters
you worked hard
then they'll begin to speak without an accent
and you will be proud to be truly Canadian

THE COUNTRY

Take the country in us
as much as we are

Breathing through silences
the uprooted air

Buttressed:
another crossing—
this I shall tell again
turning with the wheel
        our encompassed selves

At a wave length
the continent's drift
I learn to live in essences
my landscape's time
on firm ground

        —unsettled
breathings
anew

WE ARE THE SELF, ENTERING

1

I am the hand that knows the door
the hand opening—turning the knob—
pushing in
my inside self
the whole self in

I am the body walking along
absorbing walls and curtains
taking in frames
seeing myself in a picture
fixed at a window

The mind dwells on images
analyses, remembers, recalls
the past—
confronts the present
with ease

I am watchful inside
I am part outside
beyond the self
I am still mere presence
becoming movement

2

You enter, filling in
the gaps, looking, taking in
the shallow outside—
inside, noticing me:
laughing

eyes screaming—
walls and frames,
the wide horizon, a picture
tumbling down,
topsy-turvy

Suddenly the voice breaks out:
we speak to each other
muttering phrases—
bodies more than shadows

linking the sun
from inside, outside—
framed together

PATRIOT

I remind myself that I am
tropical to the bones
I blend with a temperate
carapace
hard lines form
across my face
I am anxious to make Canada
meet in me
I make designs
all across
the snow

II
...a realist's touch

AFTER ROMANCE

for Derek Walcott

1

Plagued into becoming more of myself
I travel along this dreamer's path—
Take the world as it is in me:
It is the only real place;
I am unable to conquer more of myself

This too is epistemology:
The ways of becoming ingrown,
Like one's toenails.
As I am reminded of the burnt-brick heap,
The bird alighting—
Remnant of a lost paradise

11

With a realist's touch,
I consider my father becoming grey
Shaking at his ramshackle bones

A brother: news of an imprisonment.
A night once again without sleep.
Oh, the ways of keeping vigil—

The imagination's fugitive;
I scatter grains of rice
Cockroaches scurry across a bed:
How a nephew slept the night through

Now this trying to hang the moon
From my pillow—
In a trade wind's rhythm;
I burn from all sides—
Feet and brain first.
Later, making amends,
I become a somnambulist, meandering
Through the thicknesses—

I mythologize as much as you.

RUM-RUNNING

A Maritimer's new life—
I am at the edge of my seat; water boiling
Mud slaking

A kiln's turn-around
At the city's end.
Fumes rise up
And swirl

Across the ocean, Atlantic's swell
And billow.
I taste cod
in Jamaica, Barbados, Trinidad
And Demerara—more trade.
In Newfoundland
Later, I lie drunkenly—

Wind wafting.
Whole fields of sugar-cane
And beet.
Backyard and tenement
Hear the police siren.
Now run, man!

An urchin's scampering feet,
Shirt tails flying in the wind.
Such ragged talk afterwards, scattering
Fowls, ducks.
A goat's lone grunt—

Good as a bray.
I hold on to a wad of notes
Like a tufted beard, dancing my way
To paradise.
Half-sotted, I echo disdain—
I continue to make believe

Patterning myself whole, dreams coming
Alive across the ocean, a ship canting,
Land lifting up, the fumes yet in my nostrils
My body's own heat—
I continue to rise like yeast

ISLANDS LOVELIER THAN A VISION

1

I am at the edge of the precipice, this resinous time.
The sun in me, this sustenance of flesh,
beating at the heart. I am awake, confused too.
I stare at you, face-to-face
swallowed up by something else

The tide – mistress in this forlorn place. Maybe
we shouldn't have come here. You say this
again and again.
    "It's difficult to understand the forces."
    "What forces?"
    "Keep pretending—"
    "Must I?"
    "It's no use, this disdain of ourselves."
    "I am vanquished."
    "It's an old tale. Of galleys—
men in the darkness;
of women and children, not seeing. Only the smell
of salted cod, and the incessant beating of hearts.
Look out, across the dim horizon.
A plantation forms the boundary.
A sunset of blood."
      "Macabre, no?"
      "It's a fact."
      "Will the sun continue to pulverize the body?"
      "A gormandizer of the spirit, also."
      "I refuse to give in—"
      "What else is there left for us?"

"Help me, precious one, help me with all your might, as I
fathom the mysteries of what surrounds us; as I give in
to you, day after day, here at the limits of the sea,
at earth's end. Take my hand—
   "I will."
   "Now speak, clearly, this language too is ours."
   "I will chant the sea in your ears."
   "That's not enough."
   "It's a burning bit in my life."
   "You etch, foam-white."
   "I cannot understand any longer. The pain
is too much."

Another high wave, rising up like a skyscraper.
The sun glinting at the tips of the horizon,
reclining at my elbow.
I am blacker. Together we have created,
you have created...
   "Do not doubt me.
   It's not the time for hesitation."
   "The moon, in me, also. The tide's hurling."
   "Ah, more of this breaking up, going on with
a broken hull, like a symbol."
   "Feeble as you are—
how can I understand you?"
   "We will survive yet."

Outside, a wet wind. Drying up once again,
I look around in dismay.
The sea's continual, restless beating.
The far horizon
bending over, as of a rock. A boulder
suddenly at my elbow.
In this cave, the bombardment continues.
The elements threaten to fill us up—
The sky,blacker.
How I want to live.
The self wanting to live.
Please, the silence...it's all we have.
Then.
Continue to dream, to imagine a life
with eyes closed.
Remember the next day
when the crescent moon raises its head.
A bloodied sun no more, coursing
through your life—
at the limits of the skin.
"This truth coming from your lips
makes me mute."
"In this, hear us.
The sea's hum, hear us."
"This cave, overwhelming."
"Further noises, I believe."
"The day is far removed, you are far removed.
This tide, our strength.
All will collapse."

IV

Distantly, a dog baying. Ululations,
this night-time. What's this, dear one?
Oh, God—I will bear my chafe—
in silence, when birth comes.
I will surrender always,
to parturition
A wound, crescendo in my midst.
"Do not give up—
hold on tightly to the mast.
Swim in your own blood if you must."
I continue to feel the pressure.
Please understand, it's no fun any longer,
this whacking at the seasons—
saccharine-sweet, falling to the ground.
Joints and sockets. This is all I can offer,
like an afterbirth.
I am wretched at the bones. Squeeze me all out
like a tube...
The light takes over.
Zinc-white clouds scudding by.

V

This flower of your smile. These islands, letting us go.
My continuing lightness. My spirit flying,
joining the tips of the waves together.
The body floating independently
like a barge.

      You in me; I, you, a song. Tremor of a wave.
A choir of voices. Cornucopia and abundance—
this happening at once.
      I cry out, in further exultation; this—
my disappearing act.
      Only waves, whiteness: heart beating, lapping.
      Rising and falling.
      Pulsation.
      I am happy.
      Take my hand, lead me away.

BALLAD WITHOUT SORROW

For you who walk
The streets in penury,
I give you skyscrapers
I bring the whole sky down,
Shower you with billows

For you who brace
Against the inside pain
I turn cafeterias
Upside down,
Hurl fruit trees
From endless orchards
With a spite

I embrace you at nights
While still rampant
In the dark,
Lighting candles
To look at your face,
Dressing your wounds
Self-inflicted
As they are.

Even if you scorn my attempts,
I will persist, call upon
The sun to dry your clothes
When you're wet.
I will blow the breath
Out of my lungs
To keep you warm

I will hold your hands
To guide you along.
Together we will survive
The next day, answer
Calls from outsiders:
We will refuse to dwell
In hollow caves—

My precious one

LENIN PARK, HAVANA
(July 14, 1982)

My camera flashes upon the variegated faces
Amidst the general activity
Of building, establishing—
How eager they are, these hands, bodies—
Nine—, ten— and eleven-year-olds
Bustling about without weariness—
Only a restrained air of the carnival
Of the young
This summer

I will speak.
"*Hola*," in bare Spanish
Eager to find out how the socialist man
Or woman can transform a state;
In command's way, they seem not to mind—
Innocence has its own currency, as I watch
A young girl driving a tractor,
A boy milling rice; another, refining sugar

Will they ever starve, as they pay tribute
To José Marti, Fidel Castro, or whoever else
Will be then?
Or will some stalwart spirit
Among them, given to brooding—
Later high on culture, insist on the right
To be free beyond bread?

Doubtful as I am, I banter, smile,
My camera snaps again, left and right—
Black hair bordering beautiful
Dark and brown faces—I love you all!
A hybrid breed chockful of Latin air—
Among you, perhaps, are eager dancers,
Singers, poets—how elegantly you proclaim
An island in the pulsation of your bodies,
In the greater exaltation of spirit yet to come
Far beyond Castro or Marti

MUSEUM

In the mountains of Peru
they bury their dead
in caves
the natives continue
to whisper secrets
to fill a century

ice now—
and this lone boy
slipped down
to his death—
still there,
frozen he lies

like elephants
around Moscow
lying in deep freeze
for over
a million years

DUBIOUS FOREIGNER

As there is no doubt
　　where I come from

I answer to all the mistrust
　　you let out
　　　　onto myself

A dollar-value citizenship card
　　bulges out
　　　　against my hide of skin

I repeat history
　　to myself
　　　　once in a while—

my feet spread out
　　against a liana sun
　　　　—swinging against the horizon

belching out the past
　　with Asia & Africa
　　　　in my ears

Next, iridescent & emerald
　　as the waves
　　　　I acknowledge the pattern

answering to myself
　　in Canada—
　　　　with crabgrass

on snowy virginal
　　ground

THE IRISH

for Claire

You said it too—
you have also been colonized

You could have joined Sinn Fein—
telling me of attending school
with Ian Paisley's daughter
instead
    I am hardly impressed

saying how he used to pick her up
each afternoon after school
such duty
    then about the letters
you received from your childhood
sweetheart—
(Paddy White)
from old Campbell College
and Beckett's words:
of such boys being the cream of Belfast—
"rich and thick"

How, together in Canada
we watch distantly,
amidst the plague of cholera
after a long voyage across
the Atlantic,
escaping potato famine
how—despite the Donnellys—
our dreams are tied
solidly together

CAMEO

This is not Normandy
I am French to the core nevertheless
I remember my Paris apartment
Oh, I am so homesick....don't get me wrong—
I've come to Canada because I want to travel:
I want to do things before I get old.

I came here, I'm working for a family.
They're in the government: they don't do things.
The man—he's ugly!
The woman's kind though;
I love the child. He loves me, too.
Each day we go for walks.
Maybe I will miss him when I leave
After the year is over.
But I came to Canada because
I wanted to see what it's like to live in North America.

I am an anarchist, you see
I know politics.
I am against materialism
I am for ecology.
Against the bomb
Am I happy? You ask
No, it is not necessary to be happy
But I am at peace with myself, more so
Than when I was eighteen or nineteen.

You know, sometimes I think you are pretentious
You think you are an artist, no?
You know what Jacques Brel said?
He said—
Everything I do, others can do too.
What do you think, eh?
Maybe I am too critical.

You see, I am against failure
I never want to fail.
I grew up without parents.
My father, he was shot in Dien Bien Phu:
He died two years later.
I was very young; I hardly remember him.
I grew up in an orphanage.
My mother had left us soon after.
Later I moved from home to home;
Maybe that's why I am bitter.

I like you, you see.
I think you're interesting.
Maybe you're kind as well:
But it's hard to tell about men sometimes—
They use women, don't they?
Some women are like that, too.
Yes, I understand.
How can I really be happy these days.
You? South American, no?
I'm reading Gabriel Garcia Marquez's
Cien Anos de Soledad.
Maybe you want to read it, too.
What do you think?
No?

VOZNESENSKY

You, Andrei Voznesensky, what is Russia
all about?
Tell me with fury on your tongue—

Let the Russian words roll out.
Does mysticism
Still surround the Russian soul?

You, *tovarish*, tell me why you're so calm tonight?
Why formalism still means so much to you?

I understand your once nearly committing suicide;
You, then a dissident

Now I suppose I forgive your interest
In Margaret Trudeau
Being here in Ottawa

(November 13, 1982)

RATTLESNAKE ANNIE

In this small town, here in Czechoslavakia,
on a week's vacation
    after two months of hard work
you went there—
    & found everyone so interesting
to talk to.
A glimpse of their life
you, from Slagelse, Denmark—
you noticed the small amount of goods
    in the stores—
but everyone is employed you say.
    And you liked the special smell of
    cigarettes the men smoked

And there was this bluegrass concert
    not far off, in that town—
    but since Rattlesnake Annie
(an Indian woman) sang with the band
    it was fine—

normally, that   isn't allowed

OJIBWAY

Tell me, Larry,
who have you conned
next—
selling fake Indian artifacts
in Toronto?

Another trip
back home
& still spending your
money on booze
in Longlac/picking
a fight with your
      girlfriend

she comes after you
like a dog
you make up/fight again
another long round
of booze
      & depression

Panhandle
for a while
then shoot pool
at Trapper Lake
where you are for
the season/planting
trees

That night

beside my bunk
you snored heavily
next morning
you painstakingly
made a sandwich—
        a dozen slices
piled high
(again the artist!)

The trees by now
have grown tall

The ground still swirls
under your feet/the artifacts
remain admired
like a dead moose's eyes

III

... in a limbo world

DINNER
for Keith Lowe

1

Responding to your invitation—
the doctor was there

We exchanged pleasantries:
Old memories, like beating clothes
by a wayside river.
Remember the English girl
who came, with whom you climbed
           Blue Mountain peak

It was unnatural at the time—
the hurricane startled you

The doctor— he said
he could have done it with zest—
he a Queen's scout—perhaps the first Chinese
in the Canadian Armed Forces

2

Harvard at eighteen, what else shaped your experience
while I remained in a ghetto, nursing the rage
of sleeping in a carton-box in grandmother's cake-shop
with bootleggers all around

Later in the American Civil Rights movement
you talked loudest:
we are all visible—
your demands, their behest

3

Neither of you speak Chinese—
Jamaica's continuing remembrances
by Cartier Street in a capital's
downtown's winter—
we eat salmon and rice; you, returning
to Toronto the next morning, then to Jamaica—
again to hear of murder!

I contemplate taking you to a burlesque:
your last night—her navel level with your eyes
the sheer cornucopia of her thighs

in Ottawa

INVASION

1

I am a disinterested admirer
Telling you this no doubt is inflammatory
Let the territory remain sacrosanct—
For how long?

We are partakers, defilers, possessors
Where we are heading is another matter

2

The old man wanders along, his beard touching
Soft ground; from shore to shore he moves
Desiring to cup the waves in his palms
The woman points her nipples at the moon
Daughters and sons are everywhere

These too are crossings
Do not forget—

In the fastnesses, life goes on
I am telling you this for us to be happy
For us to make amends in the darkest night

3

It is of a loved one that I think most
Who breathes his last
After a bomb-blast

Let me speak of hope
Of the desire to bring the islands together
Like solid dreams
Like a blanket thrown over the dead
To cover shame

JUNTA

In the armpit of sun
in the wake of body's heat
spread out like galvanized
zinc sheets
in the mirage of rice paddies
and whole fields
that burn
I hold you ransom

Water seeps through
I am wet with fury
I hold on to your mouth
lips puckered
stopping the words
I raise an accusing finger
how do we nourish the body
where do we go from here?

I am in a limbo world
I am not on your side
of the border

I am still wet—
almost dry
I hold a fist at the sky
I wait your answers
in blood

SUGAR & CAULDRON

This is new country—
Sun & topsoil,
the country boiling;
we talk to each other
        in the domain,
the outer reaches
        where expectation
is rife

Changeover one last time
        I heave with skin,
flesh—
        I'm still etched with the sun,
body sweltering
        overtaking all else

Discovering myself anew—
        voice throbbing,
drum-like
        waving the banner
thrashing through the thickets
        my body laid out
finally

This frenzy of soil
        and warning...
a conflagration
        of spirit—
meeting at the outer reaches:
        a molasses time
all around

SIX CARIBBEAN POEMS

i)   Sun

A greenyard sun
spreading out
blades sharp
as razor—
everywhere
iridescence—
hands cut
bleeding
red/red clotting
juice sticky wet
all dried up
sore and raw

ii)   Banana Day

One stalk down
another to go
hands big-big
machete-man
walking away,
crunch of blade
on stalk & counting
the hours,
labour done;
afternoon sun
declining,
the body's sweat
still dripping;
a tree about to fall—
coming down, slowly
then a heavy crack—
          thunder
the entire sky
          falls
                    down

iii)   Fields

In the fields again,
mixing with sugar-
cane, life evolving;
so goes the hoary
Indian myth, man's
evolution—
Arawak still in my
midst, chopping away,
feeling the heat, with
thick blades
at my sides. Trash
all about, ash on
my body, sticky.
A mask-man, now
ready to beat pan,
playin' de tune
in my head, raw an'
ready, heaving with sun,
sky on my shoulder—
skin more topsoil

iv)   Quest

Fruits thicker than
hands, larger than
elbows: paw-paw,
sapodilla; juice sweet—
sweet in us:
blood of body, rind
of skin, all mottled;
a bitter-sweet life—more
fruits in my midst: mangoes,
oranges, semitoos.
A life among leaves,
climbing farther up,
hailing the coconut
tree of sky

v) Legacy

Bolder
    each moment
laughing loudly
in the open,
pods exploding—
too soon now
to be jumping over
the moon—
these songs all around,
remember the stage,
calypso/steelband—
or ascend the tree
of knowledge; ah,
no one really cares.
Words uttered, spirited
out, the body moving
with limbo stride—
further holding
the sun at bay

vi) Politics

A life without
much ease;
so succumb to
corruption;
get rich on the side.
Sway the peasants
as you please—
clap-trap ideology.
I am further non-aligned;
this promise of manna
from heaven—
more rhetoric, walking
along gold-dust streets
with El Dorado
strides—
a politician with a gun—
Start counting, brother;
run faster than Quarrie
or Crawford—
it ain't fun!

REQUIEM

de water coming out o' his skin
he leapin' aroun'

he passin' time
with crabs
eyes lookin' back at him
water touchin' sand

makin' furrows all
about his skin
clothes wet
T-shirt wringing

mouth wiped clean of salt—
water, lips curled in—
he watchin' and waitin'
he beginnin' with a song
about how little
he understands life—

he livin' out his time
makin' peace with water
only earth left behind
his one-pound fist-body
sinkin' down
like a lost ship

DIASPORA

You presume to know
more of the world
than you were prepared for

New York— you transformed
And transforming. Breathing
fully, trying to understand
    the sum of a life

Making music with your telephone
    tongue. Highrises. Cars zooming by.
Night school & getting your B.A.

Standford next. A dream coming true.
    You're still a union man
championing workers' right in the big city

Surprises to follow—
    in the familiarity
of memorable colloquialisms

LANDSCAPES

Walking out early
This morning—
And dreaming

Of riding
The waves
Shadows rounding out

A palm tree—
Hot sand under
My feet

Where an old woman
Scours the neck
Of the sea

Squinting
With shrimp
In her eyes

Sprays rise up
More wind—
Leaving behind

How much else
Is there to give
I needed your prompting

A heart in throes—
A mother & child
Heaving with plenty
In my midst

The ground
Swirls
Its ease

PASSION PLAY

Heart, take me there where I know myself—
Take me to the wide rivers once again
Brown, the waters, the plying raft
The shadow of the hand, mighty oars; take me
Where I am also the flower bursting out
From a ribbed cage—
The boa-constrictor uncoils malevolently

Heart, make me bolder yet even as I am near hunger,
Same as the man who will cry *jump, jump,*
From a high window
To find salvation, the shanty-town deep in his ears—
Help me make a living out of nothing

Heart, I am the kernel of the coconut-seller's dream,
In this narrow street, in an old colonial town—
I offer you a sacrifice, this jelly, precious water,
My blood: I will sate your appetite for a while
You will not dream of bread any longer
In the darkest night –
All the world's orchards will be ours

Heart, let me tumble down with rain-clouds
Crossing the river again, looking with rainbowed eyes
I enter a cave here, where I can survive longest—
My spirit whole, body bent, prostrate
A new beginning; hear me, oh heart—
Help me keep intact the fire in my eyes

SONATA

I am in the frenzy of another life
I give the village hands and legs

I listen to everyone's surprised
laughter, as I keep talking
in dreams—

I fail to understand why I am
like this; I'm held ransom
once more

eyes and ears next—
no longer mine;
I shout with a loud voice

my heart stops
I turn around and burrow
deeper into myself

this pact goes on
from day to day
as I continue to live

in bones—
to salvage a life

IV

... marred with upheaval

HALLOWEEN

She phoned
and talked
about the red moon
rising

       Earlier
my students stirred
me with fears about
the Ku Klux Klan

(winter approaching
a hard sun disappearing
leaves changing
colour)

A life withering too;
I'm losing a lover;
another
I'm trying to persuade
to write her memoir

(she's just been separated
from her husband—
finally having
the courage
to stand up to him)

I tell her the moon
is a bag of blood

We joke about the season's
aphrodisaic
more men are turned on
by it
     she says

Tomorrow
the white linen sheet
of clouds
the night's turning
blacker

I insist that I'm here
to stay

ELOQUENCE

This lopsided walk,
Eating away at the soles
And making longer strides

Shadows all around,
At the start—
Eyes livid
Talking to the sun
And pulling yourself
Up a rafter

Next, caked dirt on your hands,
Nails. Body coming to this,
Mouth set in a grimace

With all the vagrants
You begin to disappear
From memory, slowly...
Here I am touched
By your semblance

As I walk along at Confederation Heights
In Ottawa's
Bright and summery day

ONE MAN'S WAR

Take note: I'm not preternaturally inclined
to believe in the war of human beings;
this is the onslaught, words lashed out at first
as a man vocally extends himself,
prehistoric in stride
and struggling through the dark

I watch him being wieldly, man with whiskers,
Himmler or Hitler; he breathes hard,
his tongue wagging,
then knotted as in barbed enclosures.
Trapped, death echoes a fulsome rapture—
travesty of an ever-present Belsen or Auschwitz.

He recounts with familiar strides,
picking out emblems of bones,
his own glamorous ways—
and dismissing the rest of us. So it appears
to this former soldier, warrior, beckoning all wars—
his tongue still rolls out thunder.

He prepares himself for the final assault,
throwing his hands above his head, glaring.
He echoes, blasts the rest of us.
He understands the drama of previous wars best.
I aim to outlast him, my quiet's victory
being catharsis from the start.

NIGHT TRAIN

(For Joanne: in California)

From *gare du nord*
in Paris
we leave
on this night train

    I lie in your lap
amidst the sonorous hum
of the train's chug-chugging
as our historical minds
recreate Dunkirk

    muffled shells
& bayonets stifling
the cry of a child
in the dark

O mother of us all
the father in me lies
half-sleeping
in this constant clang
    of iron & steel

Your eyes open—
you keep a perfect vigil
of the disappearing past

        (Paris, July 1978)

AMERICAN WOMAN

You send me a postcard
from St. Martin D' Heres
in France
    where you lived
in the foyer
of a Catholic dormitory
that summer

It wasn't a life
fit for a feminist
    and even though
you learnt French—
it was still the absence
of men in your life—
    uppermost

You are tranquil, however
    reminding me
to read the review
    of your book
in the *New York Times*
    while I make a promise
to better understand
    the uses of gender

PARTNERSHIP

(or a dream)

I continue to give you arms & legs
Your body holds out against dismemberment
You turn and look at me without a grimace
I offer bandages without so much as an apology

We continue our old game, looking at each other
with myriad eyes from false sockets,
exchanging hearts & lungs.
After a while I put my trophies in a bag
and sling it across my shoulder—

time for the wandering again;
I leave you behind with a look of distress
You follow with a handful of flowers,
your octopus limbs stretching out, trying
to embrace me

And I keep looking back at the sun
shining down upon us; I keep hoping that this
will not last forever. Your tentacled arms
will soon be all around me—

and I begin squirming, disappearing
from life altogether

FAREWELL

Our blood no longer runs in the same vein
You hold on to reason with a passion
I make amends with water falling—
Our pith and cambium hearts

No longer relevant. On our different worlds,
You try to decipher the heiroglyphic
Concept. The philosopher's stone glitters from afar

We will continue to write letters, brother.
I will begin with a farewell song of praise
All will be well in Canada

Until old Athens is ready to burn her acropolis
Because you have stayed away for so long

MAGIC ROBOT

You came into my life
with a shiny newness
answering questions
about the universe

I was only nine
or ten—
but I knew your style
was false

      when the arm broke

Then your answers drew blood
I could only be amazed
as the world
was suddenly

      without a centre

You spun on glass
like an ineffectual
dancer—
so time went by

      marred with upheaval

one-armed
      one-armed

WOLFE ISLAND, ONTARIO

You have made a pact
with the lake
as pickerel & pike
come up to round off
your life

For seventy years or more
you breathed,
heavily, as the waves
beat against the island

Now the girls attending Queen's
humour you with Maritime jest,
flouncing their shapely
eighteen-year-old bodies
—you continue fishing

They tell you about the boys
in their lives, of riding
around the island
& wishing to take them
by surprise

You smile, ask questions
about the world—
They laugh; you look down
into the lake, seeing all
the knotted things;
rock-bottom for a while,
you imagine a youth—
a life never fully spent

The girls leave now
they enter the ferry,
passing the old fort,
the military college—
you wave steadily,
like an awakened dreamer

when all is gone you empty
your blood & guts into the lake
the fishes make patterns
all across your life

EXILES: A SEQUENCE

(#101)

He stole into the sun
and garnered himself a place

It was so from the beginning;
with the seasons in his dreams—
he expresses the drama of himself

—describing events to everyone
living alone in the cold & ice.

His body grows old, as he loosens up,
mouth opening in the eternal longing
for more sun. He walks along,
Oedipus-like—

sweltering with leaves glazed,
the omen of windows rattling:
shingled all around

Such solid remnants—
offering hope because of where
he came from, whence he must return

(#102)

Pretending to be part of the self
he followed you to the source
the sun in his heart—

still the source of his dream,
overturning one more time,
he makes amends, listening

with cocked ear, mouth
opening like a tunnel...
everything in his grasp

He talked as if abundance
was everywhere. Obsidian again,
he remembered his own tragic fate—

how he once nurtured the desert,
chattering at the edge of the sea
when the sirens came

voices locked in his head,
memory of a madness,
caves form as in a dream—

he withdrew into himself
singing, until peninsulas
crumbled at his feet

(#103)

How they were conceived
    making much ado about little
        talking to the banner

in his heart

Brandishing a sword, mouth
    opening, spilling out
        seeds, the dream

still with him

Legs spread apart
    the limbo sun
        underneath, beating

out rhythm

Still talking loudest
    he remembers a life—
        memory & hope

taking over

Everything as in a war
    muttering words on soft
        ground, wounds dry up—

such solid imprints

(#104)

Hounded to the dust—
travail with him,
he still talks of pride
of place, of whence
he came—
whence he must return

Shadows long and grey,
teeth jutting over
the hard lip,
genuflecting—

gripping stones, pebbles,
looking for further
spaces in between—
a life's long
face, grimacing

        then,

rolling over
in the dust—an
ass's bray,
feet & hands
intertwined

he breathes his last
at the sound
of thunder—
drama of the insides

one last time
he looks up before
lowering his gaze
to the horizon
in fulfilment of
his dream, or a
life of prophecy

(#105)

Breathing out
        sun coruscating—
        this and more

he looks back, re-creating
        memory: the debris
        taking over

potsherd, hide, mottled
        skin; shells, soft
        ground; scampering

waves. All secrets to himself,
        the feathered sea
        riding along

Pegasus again, the tunnel
        wind berating,
        arid fields

in his midst. The sun diving
        under on its own—
        melding with time

being one with the elements
        the solidness of dust,
        sand, pebbles

(#106)

The self in green,
myriad shapes—
life reborn

nurturing
the island
and the sea

fish everywhere;
a heart racing
to the beginning—

galleys, slave ships, the
crossing's hard luck,
stretched

to a mammoth grimace;
prisms mocking—
a rainbow

making amends,
with blood:
vermilion & russet

hues—
a crescent tongue
further magic

with words
shadowing the sun's
emblazoned eyes

(#107)

Pretences being less
the self asking for more—
    the imaged bird in his midst,
hands outlining the shadow,
    empty spaces everywhere;
meeting again without much fuss:
    the ground hardening, fallow fields
shooting out as in a miracle

Such essences in his life,
making magic out of words,
    retracing the sun again, horoscope
    already drawn, body yearning
to be at one with you & holding
    the blade of the sword—
pretending seasons existed
    only with the last romance